PALEO

A Simple Start To

The 7-Day Paleo Diet Plan For Beginners

Written by ALISHA ABBOTT

Published by "Aston Publisher"

Paleo

Paperback ISBN-13: 978-1512338737

Table Of Contents

What is Paleo Diet? Is It Effective?

Most of the diets nowadays will preclude you from optimum intake of protein, carbohydrates as well as meat consumption. Before going to get a diet plan make sure you've all the details of it especially when it comes to Paleo diet.

Paleo diet is so called as "Hunter Gatherer Diet" and possesses seeds, meat, nuts, vegetables as well as fruits. The diet resembles to the diet what our ancestors had in the past to maintain the schedule of mild to moderate active routine regarding meals. However, some of the products you need to preclude yourself from are processed foods, dairy products, fatty meat as well as grains and other food stuff that are rich in carbohydrates and fats as they weren't available to eat back then. Paleo diet seems to have certain restrictions but you still got a lot of good and healthy options with tasty recipes that you would definitely want to consume with your family.

Seafood, nuts, vegetables, fruits and meat are the main product in the Paleo diet because it focuses mainly on protein. Majority of the veggies you can have in the diet except potatoes because of their richness in carbohydrates. Most of the sports man and athletes also pursue the same diet to get going and be fit with their schedule. This could be the main dish as well as a side dish along with any other meal and it proves why Paleo diet is effective and efficient for health.

Bad eating habits or excessive eating can cause digestive disorders as well as allergies which include grain and dairy items. The only thing that makes this diet very popular, hygienic and wholesome is that, its dairy and wheat free containing low fats and high fiber in the meal resulting boost in energy level.

This diet is effective for those who really want to have boost in the energy level and slim down their bodies simultaneously as well as stay away from cancer as well as heart diseases.

Paleo Diet & Fat Loss:

It's always difficult to achieve a unique, smart and wholesome physique. It's been the problem for decades now to go through tough schedules to achieve smart and healthy body. Once you set the pattern for yourself to run through the hurdles then you'd be able to lose weight but most of the time people put on weight again very abruptly when they disrupt their daily schedule even for couple of days. One will get fed up of this forever diet plan which most of the guru's would prefer to suggest to their clients and motivate them for struggling hard and even harder.

What these people need is more natural and un-processed diet to give them exactly what they need in their food in the form of nutrients, vitamins as well as minerals resulting energy. They need to keep things balance and make sure that whatever goes inside the body must come out preferably twice the amount that they took. Veggies and other mixture e.g. natural foods such as seeds as well as nuts are healthy, beneficial and will make things better for the body to keep it going precisely. Avoid processed food and other products e.g. beverages, butter, cheese and creamy milk that can help you put on more weight and can devastate all the efforts that has been done to reduce weight.

Paleo is the most effective and healthy diet to lose weight conveniently when it combines with proper exercise schedule that will nurture your body and will help you lose excessive fats easily.

Paleo Diet & Stronger Health:

To spend your moments enthusiastically and more energetically then Paleo is the right choice. It will help you overcome all the things that are lacking in the body and will motivate you to do things that you really want to perform. It will also help overcome dizziness and sickness of the elderly age period and will change the life for good.

Go for the food that you simply think is best for you in the list of Paleo diet and eat it until you feel not to eat anymore of it. Why Paleo diet is important for us?? If we look at our ancestors they consumed a lot of meat, fruits, vegetables, berries and fish without any of the grains involved in it but since ages we are consuming the same food that's the reason our body got addicted to it.

Through various surveys and reports archeologist proved that the decline in human health has been noticed just because of change in the diet. As compare to our ancestors they were a lot more taller and stronger moreover, had less diseases and sudden deaths so they were able to survive for longer just because of the food they had.

Furthermore, unique ways of cultivation and growing the corps through revolutionized chemicals caused devastation of the environment along with minimizing the forests and building industries instead. Ages ago we initiated to consume food which we didn't have adaptation to e.g. beans, potatoes, corn and grains etc resulting in expanding diseases e.g. constant lack of energy, allergies and diabetes as well. Those who consume natural foods still having strong physique and healthy life.

Why Go Paleo?

Go paleo because it's natural diet and it means to avoid all un-necessary and processed food. Some communities like to have gluten free diet because of the hyper sensitivity that's why Paleo is the best option for the daily diet schedule to go for.

One of the core advantage of this diet is you'll get hassle free schedule regarding calories even if you eat 4 times a days.

Paleo Diet

A good Paleo diet is one that would contain more of:

Fiber, micronutrients, vitamins, proteins, good fat, and minerals

Less Of:

Sodium and Carbohydrates

There are do's and don'ts for everything then why not for Paleo diet. The do's that you need to pursue in the form of foods are eggs, fish, meat and other plants to help your body with nutrients. Other items that are included in the list namely liver, skin, meat and the rest parts of the animal. Remember you've to have very minimum amount of sodium in your diet or would be much better if you say "NO" to sodium.

The Do's Also Include:

Grass fed or pasture raised meat, Fresh fruits and vegetables, Coconut water, Eggs, Fish/ sea food, Oil (olive, flaxseed, avocado, coconut), Nuts/seeds, Herbal tea like ginger, Fermented food like sauerkraut, chamomile, nettle, peppermint can be had in moderation.

The Don'ts Include:

Salt, rice, cereal grains, legumes, yogurt, cheese, butter, dairy like milk, add sugar, potatoes, packaged food and processed food. Vegetable oils like peanut oil, Crisco, sunflower, margarine, Juices, soda, coffee, tea, Alcohol

You Can Have In Moderation:

Unrefined sea salt, dried fruit, raw honey and chocolate.

The red alert during this is, diet is to stay away from beverages and replace it with plain water, fruit juices or fruit shakes without adding sugar to it.

How Can I Start Living The Paleo Lifestyle?

To change the food schedule abruptly is really a hassle and especially when you want to go on diet. The good thing about this diet is you don't have to shorten the variety of food, just replace it with better alternative. Gradually replace the items that you have in your Paleo diet with current diet schedule, it can take few days but ones you think you can pursue the routine without any hurdle then stick to it and make it a habit.

The changes with your lifestyle that would affect for good are:

- Sunlight exposure to have sufficient vitamin D.
- Get yourself busy with activities e.g. jumping, lifting, swimming, running, walking, roping etc.
- Gardening is another natural activity that you need to go for.
- Get sufficient sleep at least 8 hours a day.

Benefits:

By eating natural food you will automatically feel the boost in energy and will feel more enthusiastic as well as healthier compare to the time were consuming processed food. Moreover, you'll feel more improvement in terms of strengthen hair, fair skin and a lot more.

How Can This Cookbook Help You?

You will have all you need to start on the road to better health. You'll also be treated to delicious recipes in 5 recipe categories that are breakfast, lunches, salads, dinners and desserts for the most finicky eater in your friends and family.

It includes simple and easy recipes with step by step instructions and a 7 day paleo diet plan for beginners. You will find everything you need to get you to that healthy place you want to be.

Paleo Diet Recipes

Paleo Breakfast

Silver Dollar Pancakes

Ingredients

- 3 large eggs
- Water (1 tbsp)
- Vanilla extract (1 tbsp)
- Honey (2 tbsp)
- Almond flour (1 ½ cups)
- Baking powder (¼ tsp)
- Coconut oil for cooking
- Sea salt (¼ teaspoon)

Directions

Heat oil in a skillet over medium high heat.

Blend honey, water, vanilla and eggs.

Add salt, almond flour and baking powder and combine thoroughly.

Pour the batter circularly to form pancakes and cook on each side for about 2 minutes.

Serve and enjoy.

Post-Workout Paleo Breakfast Bake

Ingredients

- 6 eggs
- Dried thyme (½ tsp)
- Garlic powder (½ tsp)
- Paprika (½ tsp)
- Salt and pepper to taste
- 3 roughly chopped onions
- 4 sliced mushrooms
- Crumbled leftover Turkey patties (¼ pound)

Directions

Preheat the oven to 350 degrees Fahrenheit.

Greased 8x8 glass Pyrex baking dish.

Mix all the ingredients in a medium bowl and shift to the baking dish.

Bake for about 40-45 minutes and then serve.

Spinach Omelet

Ingredients

- Minced chicken (2 ounces)
- Handful of baby spinach, chopped
- Pepper and salt to taste
- 2 beaten eggs
- Butter (1 tsp)
- Cayenne pepper to taste

Directions

Put the frying pan on the stove and melt butter in it.

Add chicken and cook until golden brown.

Flavor it with pepper and salt.

Mix spinach, eggs and cayenne pepper and then shift to the pan to cook for about 60 seconds.

Serve and enjoy.

Coconut Porridge

Ingredients

- Flaxseed golden meal (1 tbsp)
- Honey to taste
- Almond flour (2 tbsp)
- Vanilla (1 tbsp)
- A pinch of salt
- Organic shredded coconut (¼ cup), unsweetened
- Coconut milk (2/3 cup)

Directions

Put the frying pan on the stove and heat coconut milk in it.

Then add all the ingredients and cook on low until thick.

Top with honey and almonds and serve.

Paleo Banana Strawberry Breakfast Cookies

Ingredients

- Chopped raisins (2 tbsp)
- Chopped pecans (2 tbsp)
- Diced strawberry (2 tbsp)
- Baking powder (½ tsp)
- Sea salt (¼ tsp)
- Vanilla (½ tsp)
- Nutmeg (1 tsp)
- Cinnamon (½ tsp)
- 2 medium eggs lightly beaten
- 2 bananas, mashed
- Unsweetened shredded coconut (½ cup)
- 6 whole dates soaked and pitted in hot water
- Almond butter (½ cup)
- Coconut flour (¼ cup)

Directions

Process coconut, almond butter and dates by using food processor.

Add baking powder, vanilla, eggs, salt, cinnamon and shredded coconut and pulse for about 30 seconds.

Shift the mixture to the bowl and softly fold in raisins, strawberries and pecans.

Take the parchment paper lining with a cookie sheet and scoop the dough by tablespoon on it.

Press each cookie and bake for about 15 minutes at 350 degrees Fahrenheit until golden brown.

Paleo Grain Free Baked Porridge

Ingredients

- Unsweetened coconut (1 cup)
- Crushed pecans (1 cup)
- Cinnamon (1 ½ tsp)
- Sea salt (1 tsp)
- 2 eggs
- Vanilla (1 tsp)
- Raw honey (¼ cup)
- Milk (1 ½ cups)

Directions

Mix the wet ingredients in one bowl and the dry ingredients in the other bowl.

Then mix together and blend well.

Take casserole dish, shift the mixture to it and bake in the preheated oven at 350 degrees Fahrenheit for about 25-30 minutes.

Add milk and splash with honey before serving.

Paleo Breakfast Stir Fry Recipe

Ingredients

- Minced garlic (1 tsp)
- Spinach (4 cups)
- Leeks (1 cup), chopped
- Chopped carrot (½ cup)
- Coconut oil (1 tsp)

- 4 eggs

Directions

Put the frying pan on the stove and heat oil in it.

Whisk egg in a bowl and flavor it with salt and pepper.

Shift the egg mixture into the frying pan, make an omelet and transfer to a serving plate.

Take a separate frying pan to cook carrot, garlic and leeks in it.

Put in spinach and cook further for a minute.

Spread this mixture over omelet before serving.

Paleo Pumpkin Pancakes

Ingredients

- Pure maple syrup (¼ cup)
- Sea salt (½ tsp)
- Baking soda (½ tsp)
- Pumpkin pie spice (1 tsp)
- Flax seed (½ cup)
- Almond flour (2 cups)
- Cinnamon (1 tsp)
- Vinegar (1 tsp)
- Almond milk (½ cup)
- Coconut oil (2 tbsp)
- 4 eggs
- Pumpkin puree (1 cup)

Directions

Put the frying pan on the stove and heat coconut oil in it.

Separate the dry and wet ingredients.

Mix all the dry ingredients in one bowl and all the wet ingredients in another bowl.

Then gradually combine both the mixtures.

Drop one large spoonful into the pan and fry on each side until golden brown.

Serve and enjoy.

Eggplant With Eggs

Ingredients

- 3 medium eggs
- Pepper and salt to taste
- Coconut oil for frying
- 2 eggplants, sliced into discs

Directions

Put the frying pan on the stove and heat coconut oil in it.

Beat the eggs and dip each disc in it.

Now take out the disc, put into the frying pan and fry until golden brown.

Spicy Granola

Ingredients

- Hemp seeds (¼ cups)
- Coconut flakes (½ cup)
- Walnuts (½ cup)

- Salt to taste
- Vanilla extract (2 tsp)
- Nutmeg (2 tsp)
- Cinnamon (2 tsp)
- Coconut oil (1/3 cup)
- Almond flour (1 ½ cups)

Directions

Preheat the oven to 275 degrees Fahrenheit.

Mix all the ingredients in a large bowl and then spread on a greased baking sheet.

Bake for about 40 minutes and then allow to cool for sometime before serving.

Divine Protein Muesli

Ingredients

- Hemp protein (1 tbsp)
- Unsweetened almond milk (1 cup)
- Cinnamon (½ tsp)
- Chocolate chips (1 tbsp)
- Raw almonds (1 tbsp)
- Chopped walnuts (1 tbsp)
- Coconut flakes (1 cup), unsweetened

Directions

In a medium bowl layer coconut flakes, chocolate chips, raisins, walnuts and almonds.

Splash with cinnamon and pour over milk before serving.

Serve and enjoy.

Ultimate Granola

Ingredients

- Coconut milk (1 cup)
- Fresh berries (2 tbsp)
- Raw pumpkin seeds (1 tsp)
- Raw sunflower (1 tsp)
- Raw pine nuts (1 tsp)
- Unsalted pistachios (1 tsp)
- Slivered almonds (1 tsp)
- Walnut pieces (1 tsp)
- Pecan pieces (1 tsp)

Directions

Take a bowl and put all the seeds and nuts in it.

Add milk and berries and reserve for some time until the berries release color into the milk.

Serve and enjoy!

Tasty Apple Almond Coconut Medley

Ingredients

- 1 pinch of salt
- Generous dose of cinnamon
- Handful of unsweetened coconut
- Handful of sliced almonds
- One-half apple cored and roughly diced

Directions

Blend all the ingredients together in a blender and serve with coconut milk.

Scrambled Eggs With Chili

Ingredients

- Salt (¼ tsp)
- Coconut milk (¼ cup)
- 6 eggs
- 1 small onion, finely chopped and peeled
- Coconut oil (2 tbsp)
- 4 fresh green chilies

Directions

Beat eggs in a bowl along with salt and coconut milk and set aside.

Take chilies, remove the skin and discard the seeds.

Now put the frying pan on the stove and heat oil in it.

Put in egg mixture and scatter chilies over it.

Cook until eggs are cooked and then serve hot.

Basil And Walnut Eggs Divine

Ingredients

- Walnuts (1/3 cup), chopped
- 3 eggs
- Pepper and salt to taste
- Fresh basil (½ cup), chopped

Directions

Put the frying pan on the stove and cook eggs in it.

Add basil and cook further for a minute.

Flavor it with pepper and salt.

Remove from heat and then add walnuts while serving.

Spicy Scrambled Eggs

Ingredients

- 4 large eggs
- 3 ripe tomatoes, peeled, seeded and chopped
- Ground black pepper and salt according to taste
- 1 chile, seeded and cut into strips
- 1 medium green pepper, cored, seeded and finely chopped
- 1 red onion, finely chopped
- Extra virgin olive oil (1 tbsp)

Directions

Heat oil in a nonstick skillet and cook onion in it for about 5-6 minutes.

Put in chile and pepper and cook further for about 5 minutes until soft.

Add tomatoes, flavor it with pepper and salt and cook uncovered for about 5 to 10 minutes on low heat.

Add eggs, cover and cook for about 6 minutes until tender.

Serve and enjoy.

Spicy India Omelet

Ingredients

- Coconut grated (¼ cup)
- 4 green chili
- Oil for cooking
- 1 onion, chopped
- 3 eggs, beaten

Directions

Put the frying pan on the stove and heat oil in it.

Mix grated coconuts along with the beaten eggs, salt, green chili and chopped onion.

Pour the above mixture into the frying pan in the form of pancakes and cook on each side.

Serve!

Spectacular Spinach Omelet

Ingredients

- Cilantro (1 tbsp)
- 2 eggs, beaten
- Coconut oil (1 tbsp)
- Tomato and onion salsa (1/3 cup)
- Raw spinach (1 ½ cups)

Directions

Put the frying pan on the stove and heat coconut oil in it.

Cook spinach in it until wilted.

Add beaten eggs and cook further until the eggs are cooked.

Add salsa and splash with cilantro before serving.

Outstanding Veggie Omelet

Ingredients

- 3 scallions, sliced diagonal
- 1 carrot, matchstick cut
- 3 eggs, beaten
- 1 handful tiny broccoli
- Salt to taste
- Safflower oil

Directions

Take a skillet and heat oil in it.

Add carrots and broccoli florets and stir fry for 2 minutes.

Then add eggs and scallions.

Flavor it with salt and serve.

Spicy Spinach Bake

Ingredients

- Olive oil
- Hot pepper flakes (½ tsp)
- Pepper and salt to taste
- 1 bunch fresh spinach, shopped
- 6 eggs

Directions

Put the skillet on the stove and heat olive oil in it.

Put in hot pepper flakes.

Take a bowl, scramble eggs and then add pepper, spinach and salt.

Pour this mixture into the skillet over hot pepper flakes and cook.

When it starts to cook then flip it over.

Take it out, let it cool for some time and then eat.

Delish Veggie Hash With Eggs

Ingredients

- 4 eggs, cooked
- Fresh spinach (1 cup), chopped
- Cherry tomatoes (1 cup), halved
- Pepper and salt to taste
- Mushroom (½ cup), sliced
- Yellow squash (1 cup), chopped
- Extra virgin olive oil (2 tablespoon)
- 2 cloves garlic, minced
- Sweet white onion (¼ cup), chopped

Directions

Heat olive oil in a skillet and sauté onion and garlic for about 2 minutes.

Add chopped squash and cook for 2 minutes more.

Further cook for 5 minutes after adding mushrooms.

Flavor it with pepper and salt.

Then add spinach and tomatoes until spinach wilts and then drain.

Serve along with cooked eggs and enjoy.

Eggs, Mushrooms And Onion Bonanza

Ingredients

- 12 hard boiled eggs, peeled and finely chopped
- 12 medium white mushrooms, finely chopped
- Coconut oil (¼ cup)
- Ground black pepper to taste
- 1 medium onion, finely diced

Directions

Heat coconut oil in a pan and sauté onions in it until golden brown.

Put in mushrooms and sauté for more 5 minutes with constant stirring until softened.

Remove from the heat and let it stand for some time to cool.

Mix with eggs and pepper while serving.

Zucchini Casserole

Ingredients

- 5 eggs
- Mushrooms (½ cup)
- ½ red onion, chopped
- Pepper and salt to taste
- 3 large zucchini

Directions

Beat the eggs in a bowl along with pepper and salt.

Take a separate bowl, grate all the zucchini in it and then mix all the ingredients in a large bowl.

Heat olive oil in a skillet and add the above mixture.

Cover and cook for about 5 minutes and then bake for about 15 minutes in the preheated oven at 375 degrees Fahrenheit.

Remove and then cool for some time before serving.

Paleo Lunches

Vegetarian Curry With Squash

Ingredients

- Coconut oil (1 tbsp)
- 1 green bell pepper, sliced thinly
- A piece of fresh ginger, peeled and minced
- Coconut milk (14 ounce)
- 1 large acorn squash, seeded, peeled and cut into cubes
- Mixed raw nuts (2 cups)
- 1 medium yellow onion, diced
- Salt (1 tsp)
- 4 cloves garlic, minced
- Lime juice (2 tsp)
- Curry powder (1 tsp)
- Cilantro (¼ cup), chopped
- Cauliflower rice

Directions

Heat the coconut oil in a frying pan and sauté onion for about 5-6 minutes until golden brown.

Add salt, garlic, ginger and bell pepper and cook for one minute more.

Put in curry powder, stir to coat all the ingredients in the pan and cook for about a minute.

Add coconut milk and simmer.

Put in squash, simmer for about 20 minutes and stir occasionally.

Roast the nuts until crisp and splash over the curry.

Remove the pan from the heat; add lime juice and splash with cilantro before serving.

Egg Bok Choy And Basil Stir Fry

Ingredients

- 1 lime, juiced
- Handful of fresh basil leaves, chopped
- Bok Choy greens (1 cup), sliced thinly
- Bok Choy stems (1 cup), sliced thinly
- 2 red chiles, sliced crosswise
- 1 small onion, finely chopped
- Olive oil (2 tbsp)
- 3 eggs

Directions

Put the skillet on the stove and heat olive oil in it.

Stir-fry onions in the oil until turns brown.

Add bok choy stems and stir-fry for about a minute.

Put in beaten eggs and cook for about 2 minutes more with constant stirring.

Put in basil, lime juice and bok choy greens and stir-fry for a minute until the bok choy wilted.

Serve and enjoy.

Eggie Vegetable Stir-Fry

Ingredients

- Butternut squash (1 pound), peeled and cut into 1 inch cube.
- Green beans (1 pound), sliced into 1 inch pieces
- 3 eggs, beaten
- Coconut oil (1 tbsp)
- Black pepper (½ tsp)
- Low sodium salt (½ tsp)
- 1 small yellow onion, sliced
- 3 garlic cloves, minced
- Eggplants (1 ½ pounds), slice into 1 inch thick pieces
- 3 baby bok choy, stems removed and cut into 1 inch pieces

Directions

Heat oil in a nonstick skillet and cook onions in it for about 2 minutes until tender.

Put in garlic and cook for one minute more.

Add beans, eggplant, bok choy and pepper and salt to taste.

Cook uncovered for about 10 minutes.

Then add bok choy leaves and cook covered for about 5 minutes.

Add beaten eggs and cook with constant stirring until cooked through.

Serve!

Pomegranate Ginger Chicken

Ingredients

- Chicken breast (1 pound), boneless, skinless,
- 2 red bell peppers, seeded and diced
- Pomegranate juice (½ cup)
- Low sodium chicken stock (1 cup)
- Grated ginger (2 tbsp)
- Onion powder (1 tbsp)
- Thyme (½ tsp)
- Low sodium salt (1 tsp)
- Pepper (1 tsp)
- Extra virgin olive oil (1 tsp)

Directions

Coat slow cooker with olive oil and then put all the ingredients in it.

Cook on high for about 4 hours or 8 hours on low.

Then serve!

Buffalo Chicken Strips

Ingredients

- Extra virgin olive oil (1 tsp)
- Paprika (1 tsp)
- Garlic powder (1 tsp)
- Frank's hot sauce (2 tsp)
- Celery (½ cup), chopped
- Chicken breast (1 ½ pounds), sliced into wide strips

Directions

Coat slow cooker with olive oil and put in chicken.

Combine the rest of the ingredients until well mixed.

Shift this mixture to the slow cooker and cook for about 4 hours on high heat.

Enjoy!

Beet Creamy Soup

Ingredients

- 2 raw beets, peeled and cubed
- Water (1 cup)
- Coconut milk (1 cup)
- 1 small onion
- 2 cloves garlic
- 1 jalapeno pepper, seeded
- Lemon juice (2 tbsp)
- Hemp seeds (2 tbsp)
- Extra virgin olive oil (¼ cup)
- Chopped parsley (2 tbsp)
- Pepper and salt according to taste

Directions

Mix beets, pepper, salt, water, coconut milk, onion, garlic, olive oil, lemon juice and hemp seeds together in a serving bowls and top with parsley before serving.

Tomato And Basil Soup

Ingredients

- 4 large ripe tomatoes, peeled
- 1 celery stalk
- ½ shallot
- 1 garlic clove
- 1 ripe avocado, peeled
- 6 basil leaves
- Pepper and salt to taste
- Olive oil (2 tbsp)
- Chia seeds (2 tbsp)

Directions

Combine tomatoes, basil, salt, pepper, avocado, garlic, shallot and celery together in a blender and blend until smooth.

Pour into the serving bowls and splash with olive oil and chia seeds while serving.

Lettuce And Cucumber Soup

Ingredients

- ½ head lettuce, well rinsed and shredded
- 1 large cucumber
- 1 ripe avocado, peeled
- 1 garlic clove
- Lemon juice (1 tbsp)
- Water (1 cup)
- Coconut cream (½ cup)
- Pepper and salt to taste
- Dried oregano (½ tsp)

Directions

Put all the ingredients together in a food processor and process until smooth.

Shift to the serving bowl and serve.

Italian Chicken On Cauliflower

Ingredients

- Chicken breast (1 pound), boneless and skinless
- Frozen cauliflower florets (5 cups)
- 2 onions, peeled and sliced
- 2 green bell peppers, seeded and sliced
- Tomatoes (1 cup), chopped
- Sea salt (1 tsp)
- Oregano (1 tbsp)
- Garlic powder (1 tbsp)

Directions

Take the slow cooker, put in chicken breast and top with spices, salt and cauliflower.

Add the remaining ingredients and cook for about 4 hours on high heat.

Serve hot!

Pesto Chicken

Ingredients

- Chicken breast (1 pound)
- 1 onion, peeled and sliced
- 4 cloves garlic, chopped
- 1 red bell pepper, sliced
- Basil (2 cups)
- Cashews (1/3 cup)
- Pine nuts (¼ cup)
- Low sodium salt (½ tsp)
- Pepper (½ tsp)

Directions

Put onion, garlic, pepper, basil, cashews, pine nuts, and salt in a food processor and process to make a sauce.

Add half of the sauce into the slow cooker, put in chicken and pour the remaining sauce over it.

Cook for about 4 hours on high heat then serve.

Zucchini And Pistachio Cold Soup

Ingredients

- 3 young zucchinis, cubed
- 1 celery stalk
- Pistachio (½ cup)
- 1 avocado, peeled
- Lemon juice (1 tbsp)
- Fresh thyme (1 tsp)
- Turmeric (½ tsp)

- 1 garlic clove
- Chopped onion (1 tbsp)
- Pepper and salt to taste

Directions

Mix all the ingredients in blender and blend until smooth.

Season to taste with pepper and salt and shift to the serving bowl.

Serve and enjoy.

Hawaiian Pineapple Chicken

Ingredients

- Chicken breast (1 pound), boneless, skinless and cubed
- Ginger (1 tbsp)
- 1 red onion, diced
- 1 jalapeno, diced
- Lime juice (1 tbsp)
- Coriander leaves (½ cup)
- Pineapple (¾ cup)
- Extra virgin olive oil (1 tsp)

Directions

Coat the slow cooker with olive oil and then add chicken cubes.

Top with the remaining ingredients and then cook for about 4 hours on high heat.

Meaty Cauliflower Lasagna

Ingredients

- Cauliflower florets (6 cups)
- Lean ground beef (1 pound)
- 6 cloves garlic, peeled and chopped
- 1 onion, peeled and chopped
- Pureed tomatoes (14 ounces)
- Sea salt (1 tsp)
- Oregano (1 tsp)
- Extra virgin olive oil (1 tsp)

Directions

Coat slow cooker with olive oil and then add ground beef along with all the other ingredients.

Cook on high for about 4 hours until ready to serve

Paleo Mushroom Soup

Ingredients

- 1 onion, chopped
- Shiitake mushroom (1 pound), chopped
- Coconut oil (2 tsp)
- Sea salt to taste
- Handful of Coriander leave

Directions

Place the stock pot on the stove and heat coconut oil in it.

Sauté onion it until caramelized.

Put in mushroom and cook uncovered for about 10 minutes.

Now lower the heat and cook cover for about 10 minutes.

Garnish with coriander leaves before serving.

Guacamole Soup

Ingredients

- 3 ripe avocados
- Fresh cilantro (½ cup)
- Water (1 cup)
- Coconut milk (1 cup)
- 2 cloves garlic
- Chives (4 tbsp)
- Pepper and salt according to taste
- 1 diced tomato

Directions

Combine avocados along with chives, cloves, garlic, cilantro, coconut milk and water in a food processor and process.

Flavor it with pepper and salt and then shift to the serving bowl.

Top with tomatoes and serve.

Chicken Spicy Rice

Ingredients

- 4 chicken fillets, cubed
- 1 head cauliflower, cut into florets
- Nutritional yeast (4 tbsp)
- Vinegar (1 tsp)
- Chopped dill (2 tbsp)
- Olive oil (4 tbsp)
- Pepper and salt to taste

Directions

Pulse the cauliflower few times in a blender until ground, but do not grind completely: it should resemble rice.

Stir in vinegar, chicken fillet, nutritional yeast, salt, pepper, olive oil and dill and serve fresh.

Spinach Tart

Ingredients

For Crust

- Raw almonds (1 cup)
- Coconut oil (2 tbsp)
- 2 kale leaves
- Nutritional yeast (1 tbsp)
- Dried basil (1 tsp)
- 1 pinch low sodium salt

For Filling

- Cashews (1 ½ cups), soaked overnight

- 2 garlic cloves
- Lemon juice (2 tbsp)
- Spinach leaves (3 cups)
- Coconut oil (4 tbsp)
- 4 beef slices, grilled
- Pepper and salt to taste
- Sun dried tomatoes (1 cup)

Directions

Blend all the ingredients of the first category in a blender to make crust.

Shift to the tart and press.

Put the beef slices over it.

Now combine coconut oil, spinach, lemon juice, garlic and cashew nuts in a blender to make filling.

Flavor it with salt and pepper and pour it over the crust along with dried tomatoes.

Chill in the refrigerator for an hour and then serve.

Avocado And Tomato Stacks

Ingredients

- 2 ripe tomatoes, sliced
- 1 ripe avocado, peeled and sliced
- 2 garlic cloves
- Cilantro leaves (1 cup)
- Extra virgin olive oil (¼ cup)
- 1 pinch chili flakes
- Pepper and salt according to taste
- Lime juice (2 tbsp)

Directions

Combine chili flakes along with olive oil, garlic and cilantro in blender and blend.

Season to taste with pepper and salt.

Arrange avocado with tomato slices and cilantro sauce and splash with lime juice before serving.

Mushroom Casserole

Ingredients

For Casserole

- 2 portobello mushrooms, sliced
- White button mushrooms (1 pound), sliced
- Sun-dried tomatoes (¼ cup), chopped
- 1 shallot, chopped
- Olive oil (2 tbsp)
- Nutritional yeast (2 tbsp)
- 2 garlic cloves, chopped
- Almonds (½ cup)
- Dried basil (1 teaspoon)

For Topping

- Walnuts (1 cup), coarsely ground
- Nutritional yeast (2 tbsp)
- 1 garlic clove, chopped
- Chopped parsley (2 tbsp)
- Salt to taste

Directions

Combine mushrooms along with sun dried tomatoes, shallot, olive oil, yeast, garlic, almonds and basil in a bowl and shift to the small casserole until the topping are ready.

Combine parsley along with garlic, yeast, salt and walnuts to make topping for the casserole.

Now splash this over mushroom casserole and serve.

Parsnip "Rice" With Hemp Seed And Basil

Ingredients

- Parsnip (1 pound), peeled and sliced
- Hemp seeds (2 tbsp)
- 1 pinch low sodium salt
- Chopped basil (4 tbsp)
- 2 ripe tomatoes, cubed
- Pepper according to taste
- Olive oil (2 tbsp)

Directions

Mix hemp seeds, salt and parsnip in a food processor and process until ground, but not pulverized: it should resemble rice.

Shift to the bowl and put in olive oil, tomatoes, basil, and pepper and salt to taste. Then serve.

Vegetable Raw Pie

Ingredients

For Crust

- Almonds (2 cups)
- Cashews (½ cup), soaked overnight
- Coconut oil (2 tbsp)

- 1 pinch low sodium salt
- Cumin powder (¼ tsp)

For Filling

- Arugula leaves (2 cups)
- Shredded lettuce (2 cups)
- 1 avocado, peeled and sliced
- 1 garlic clove
- 1 green onion
- Chopped parsley (2 tbsp)
- 1 lime, juiced
- Cherry tomatoes (1 cup), halved
- Pepper and salt to taste

Directions

Take the food processor and process cumin powder, salt, coconut oil, cashews and almonds in it and then shift to the pie pan. Set aside.

Now combine lime juice, parsley, green onion, garlic and avocado to make filling.

Flavor it with pepper and salt.

Take a bowl and mix the avocado sauce along with arugula and lettuce and then pour it over crust.

Splash with cherry tomatoes and serve.

Guacamole Stuffed Peppers

Ingredients

- 2 large bell peppers, halved and then cored
- 1 ripe avocado
- 2 garlic cloves

- 1 green onion
- Chopped cilantro (4 tbsp)
- 6 cherry tomatoes, diced
- Pepper and salt to taste
- 1 pinch chili flakes
- Lime juice (2 tbsp)

Directions

Mix cilantro, salt, pepper, chili flakes, lemon juice, onion, garlic and avocado together in a blender and blend until smooth.

Put in tomatoes and spoon into bell pepper halves while serving.

Zucchini And Cauliflower Soup

Ingredients

- 1 young zucchini
- Cauliflower florets (2 cups)
- 1 small avocado
- Water (1 cup)
- 1 Garlic clove
- ½ small sweet onion
- Chopped cilantro (4 tbsp)
- Cumin powder (½ tsp)
- 1 pinch chili flakes
- Pepper and salt to taste

Directions

Blend all the ingredients for about 2 minutes in a blender until smooth.

Shift to the serving bowls. Serve, eat and enjoy!

Asparagus And Mushroom Soup

Ingredients

- 14 asparagus spears, trimmed
- 1 ripe avocado, peeled
- 1 sweet onion
- 2 clove garlic
- Water (2 cups)
- Coconut milk (½ cup)
- Olive oil (2 tbsp)
- Chopped cilantro (2 tbsp)
- Button mushroom (1 cup), sliced
- Pepper and salt to taste

Directions

Combine asparagus along with avocado, onion, garlic, water, coconut milk, olive oil and chopped cilantro in a food processor and process for about 2 minutes until creamy and smooth.

Flavor it with pepper and salt and serve in bowls along with sliced mushrooms over it.

Paleo Salads

Spicy Tuna Salad

Ingredients

- Tuna (2 cans), water packed, drained
- Black olives (1 cup)
- Green olives (1 cup), chopped
- 2 green onions, chopped
- 1 jalapeno pepper, finely chopped
- Capers (3 tbsp), rinsed
- Red chili flakes (½ tsp)
- 2 lemon, juiced
- Splash of olive oil
- 1 head butter lettuce, kale or mixed greens
- 1 avocado, sliced

Directions

Combine, black olives, green olives, tuna, onions, jalapeno pepper, caper, chili flakes and lemon juice together and mix well.

Top with greens and place sliced avocado on the top.

Serve with tortillas.

Pomegranate Salad

Ingredients

- 1 arugula lettuce, washed, dried and torn into small pieces
- 1 pomegranate, seeds removed

- Extra virgin olive oil (5 tbsp)
- 2 garlic cloves, minced
- Freshly squeezed lemon juice (2 tbsp)
- Sea salt and pepper to taste

Directions

Combine lemon juice, garlic, pepper, salt and oil together in a jar and shake well.

Now combine pomegranate seeds along with lettuce in a serving bowl and mix with clean hands.

Shake the above mixture and pour over the salad while serving.

Arugula Avocado Salad And Raisins

Ingredients

- 2 handfuls of arugula leaves, washed and dried well
- 1 avocado, cut into half, seeded and sliced thinly
- Organic raisins (½ cup)
- ½ thinly sliced Spanish onion
- 6 cherry tomatoes, cut lengthwise
- Extra virgin olive oil (6 tbsp)
- Freshly squeezed lemon juice (2 tbsp)
- Salt and pepper to taste

Directions

Mix lemon juice along with pepper, salt and olive oil together to make dressing.

Now combine tomatoes, onion, raisins, avocado and arugula leave together and top with the above dressing while serving.

Mediterranean Chicken Delish Salad

Ingredients

- 1 lemon, juiced
- 1 red onion, diced
- 1 head of romaine or butter lettuce
- Salt and pepper according to taste
- Fresh cilantro (¼ cup), chopped
- Olive oil (½ cup)
- 1 roasted chicken, shredded

Directions

Put the shredded chicken in a large bowl and add oil, cilantro, red onion, lemon, pepper and salt together.

Mix well and serve on a lettuce boat.

Chicken Basil Avo Salad

Ingredients

- Basil leaves (½ cup), stem removed
- 1 cooked boneless and skinless chicken breast, shredded
- Cherry tomatoes (1 cup), sliced
- Extra virgin olive oil (2 tbsp)
- 2 small avocado, skin removed
- Low sodium salt (½ tsp)
- Ground black pepper (1/8 tsp)

Directions

Put the shredded chicken in a mixing bowl.

Blend avocado, basil, ground black pepper, salt and olive oil together in a blender until smooth and pour it over shredded chicken along with avocado and tomatoes.

Toss to coat well.

Chill in the refrigerator and then serve.

Chicken Salad

Ingredients

For Salad

- Organic chicken (2 cups), cooked
- Fresh mint (¼ cup), chopped
- Fresh cilantro (¼ cup), chopped
- Radishes (¼ cup), julienned
- Scallions (¼ cup), trimmed and julienned
- Carrot (1 cup), julienned
- 1 small head of cabbage, shredded

For Vinaigrette

- Fresh ginger (1 tsp)
- 1 clove garlic, crushed
- 1 chipotle pepper
- Sesame oil (2 tbsp)
- ½ lime, juiced
- Vinegar (2 tbsp)

Directions

Combine radishes, scallions, carrot and cabbage together.

Splash with cilantro, mint and chicken and set aside.

Now combine the vinaigrette ingredients and drizzle the salad with it while serving.

Chicken Taco Salad

Ingredients

- Olive oil (1 tsp)
- Vinegar (1 tsp)
- Water (¼ cup)
- Taco seasoning (1 ½ tsp)
- Chicken (½ lbs), cooked and chopped
- Shredded lettuce
- Tomatoes or avocado for topping
- Sweet potato chips, crushed

Directions

First make the dressing and place in the refrigerator to chill.

Heat olive oil in a skillet and cook chicken in it.

Add taco seasoning and water and simmer for some time until liquid is gone.

Shred tomatoes or avocados and assemble lettuce along with tomatoes or avocados, chicken crushed chips and dressing.

Serve and enjoy.

Macadamia Chicken Salad

Ingredients

- Olive oil (1 tbsp)
- Vinegar (2 tsp)

- Julienned basil (2 tbsp)
- Diced celery (½ cup)
- Macadamia nuts (½ cup), chopped
- Few pinches of pepper and low sodium salt
- Macadamia nut oil (1 tsp)
- Organic chicken breast (1 lb)
- Lemon juice (1 tbsp)

Directions

Preheat the oven to 350 degrees Fahrenheit.

Drizzle a pinch of pepper and salt on chicken breast placed on the sheet tray and then bake for about half hour until cooked well.

Take out and let it stand for some time to cool.

Now shred chicken in a large bowl and add basil, dressing, celery, nuts and salt and pepper to taste.

Stir to combine and eat.

Avocado Tuna Salad

Ingredients

- Chicken breast, cooked and chopped
- Lettuce leaves of your choice
- Pepper and salt according to taste
- Mashed avocado
- Chopped almonds

Directions

Mix all the ingredients (except lettuce) together in a medium bowl and flavor to taste with pepper and salt.

Then spoon the mixture on the lettuce leaves and roll up.

Serve, eat and enjoy.

Sweet Apple Coleslaw

Ingredients

- Finely sliced white cabbage (2 cups)
- 2 medium sized carrots, shredded
- 1 apple, chopped
- 1 stalk celery, chopped
- 1 green onion, sliced thinly
- Handful of toasted sunflower seeds
- Extra virgin olive oil (¼ cup)
- Organic honey (2 tbsp)
- Freshly squeezed lemon juice (1 tbsp)
- Ground black pepper and sea salt to taste

Directions

Combine honey, lemon juice, olive oil, pepper and salt together in a jar, shake well and set aside until the coleslaw is prepared.

Mix the veggies together in a bowl, pour the above dressing over it and toss until well mix.

Splash the salad with sunflower seeds and toss again.

Store for about 10 minutes and serve.

Delicious Slaw

Ingredients

- ½ head of cabbage
- 4 carrots
- 1 onion
- Walnut oil (3 tbsp)
- 1 beaten egg
- Fresh lemon juice (1 tbsp)
- Pepper according to taste

Directions

Grate carrot, onion and cabbage and combine together until well mix.

Now mix lemon juice, walnut oil, beaten egg and pepper to make dressing.

Splash over salad and serve.

Chicken Eastern Surprise

Ingredients

For Salad

- Grilled chicken (2 cups), chopped
- 6 baby bok choy, grilled and chopped
- 2 green onions, chopped
- Cilantro (¼ cup), chopped
- Sesame seeds (1 tbsp)

For Dressing

- Fresh lime juice (2 tbsp)
- Sesame oil (1 tbsp)
- Fish sauce (1 tbsp)
- Coconut cream (2 tbsp)
- Fresh ginger (1 tsp)

Directions

Combine bok choy, chicken, onions, cilantro and sesame seeds together until well mixed.

Now put all of the dressing ingredients into the food processor and process until smooth.

Pour it over salad and toss to coat.

Let it cool for about 60 minutes in the refrigerator and then serve with more sesame seeds on the top if desired.

Artichoke Tuna Delight

Ingredients

- Diced grilled tuna (1 ½ cups)
- 1 small carrot julienned and cut into small pieces
- Finely diced red onion (¼ cup)
- 5 artichoke hearts, diced
- Capers (2 tbsp)
- 6 radicchio leaves
- Pepper and salt to taste

Directions

Combine all the ingredients (except radicchio leaves) in bowl.

Mix well and then spoon the mixture on radicchio leaves and chill in the refrigerator in an air tight container before serving.

Advanced Avocado Tuna Salad

Ingredients

- 1 avocado
- Salt and pepper to taste
- Cooked tuna (5 ounces)
- Chopped tomatoes (1 cup)
- Chopped onion (1 tbsp)
- 1 Lemon, juiced

Directions

Take a bowl, cut the avocado and scoop the middle of both halves into the bowl.

Combine with onion and lemon juice and mash together.

Stir in pepper, sodium salt and tuna and then fill the avocado halves with this mixture while serving.

Creamy Carrot Salad

Ingredients

- Carrot (1 pound), shredded
- Crushed pineapples (20 ounces), drained
- Chicken breast, shredded
- Flaked coconut (¾ cup)
- Coconut milk (8 ounces)

Directions

Mix all the ingredients together in a bowl.

Toss until well mixed.

Covered and chill in the refrigerator before serving.

Asian Aspiration Salad

Ingredients

- 1 red bell pepper, sliced
- 1 cucumber, cut into half and sliced
- 1 large carrot, cut into matchsticks
- 2 boiled eggs
- Fresh ginger juice and vinegar

Directions

Mix all the above ingredients together in a bowl and serve

Tasty Carrot Salad

Ingredients

- Olive oil (2 tbsp)
- Lemon juice (2 tsp)
- Low sodium salt (¼ tsp)
- Mustard seeds (1 tbsp)
- 5 carrots, medium
- 1 grated egg

Directions

Grate carrots in a medium bowl and toss with salt. Set aside.

Heat olive oil in a skillet and add mustard seeds.

When the seeds begin to pop then pour it over carrot.

Also add lemon juice and toss until well mixed.

Add grated egg while serving.

Paleo Dinners

Saucy Gratin With Creamy Cauliflower Bonanza

Ingredients

- 4 cloves garlic, chopped
- 2 large shallots, diced
- Extra virgin olive oil (1 tbsp)
- Fresh spinach (6 cups)
- Pepper according to taste
- Pinch nutmeg
- 1 large sweet potato, peeled and sliced thinly
- 1 medium butternut squash, peeled, seeded and diced
- Ingredients for sauce:
- Nutmeg (¼ tsp)
- Ground pepper (½ tsp)
- Sodium salt (½ tsp)
- Chicken stock (½ cup)
- Almond milk (1 cup)
- ½ head of cauliflower, cut into florets

Directions

Preheat the oven to 375 degrees Fahrenheit.

Boil water in a large pot, place steamer insert and then cauliflower florets before covering.

Steam for about 15 minutes until tender.

Drain and then put the cauliflower back to the pot.

Put in pepper, salt, nutmeg, chicken stock and almond milk and then process all the ingredients by using an immersion blender. Set aside.

Now boil water in a separate pot, add butternut squash and cook for about 5 minutes.

Drain and reserve.

Heat olive oil in a skillet and sauté garlic and shallot for about 5 minutes until tender.

Put in spinach and flavor it with pepper and salt.

Take large baking dish to assemble all the ingredients in it.

Grease the baking dish with coconut oil spray and then layered with cream sauce.

Now arrange half of the butternut squash and splash with the spinach mixture and potato.

Drizzle with cream sauce and then add the remaining half of the spinach along with the butternut squash and.

Drizzle with the remaining cream sauce.

Now add nutmeg, pepper and salt and bake for about an hour until browned.

Let it stand for some time to cool and then serve.

Sweet Potato Spiced Soup

Ingredients

- 2 large sweet potatoes, peeled and cubed
- Turmeric powder (1 tsp)
- Cumin powder (½ tsp)
- 1 pinch nutmeg

- 1 pinch cinnamon powder
- Coconut cream (½ cup)
- Water (2 cups)
- Garlic powder (¼ tsp)
- Onion powder (¼ tsp)
- Hemp seeds (4 tbsp)
- Pepper and salt to taste

Directions

Combine turmeric, water, coconut cream, garlic, sweet potatoes, cumin powder, nutmeg, and cinnamon together in blender and blend for about 2 minutes.

Season to taste with pepper and salt and then shift to the serving bowl.

Splash with hemp seeds while serving.

Roasted Bell Pepper Soup

Ingredients

- 4 roasted bell peppers
- 2 large ripe tomatoes
- ½ fennel bulb
- 4 basil leaves
- ½ red onion
- ½ lemon, juiced
- Water (1 cup)
- ½ chile pepper, seeded
- 2 garlic cloves
- Pepper and salt to taste
- Extra virgin olive oil (2 tbsp)

Directions

Take the blender and combine water along with lemon juice, chili, tomatoes, bell peppers, fennel, basil, onion, garlic and chili and blend for about 2 minutes.

Shift the mixture to the serving bowl and splash with olive oil while serving.

Black Olive Tapenade In Zucchini Boats

Ingredients

- 3 young zucchinis,
- 2 Sun-dried tomatoes
- Olive oil (2 tbsp)
- Pitted black olives (1 cup)
- Almonds (½ cup)
- 2 basil leaves
- Pepper and salt accordingly

Directions

First cut all the 3 young zucchinis lengthwise into two halves.

Then chop after removing the flesh from it.

Take a bowl, put the zucchinis in it and set aside.

Combine basil leaves along with almonds, black olives, sun-dried tomatoes and olive oil in a food process and process.

Mix with the zucchini flesh after processing.

Fill the zucchini with the above mixture and serve.

Mint Zucchini Pasta With Pistachio Crumble

Ingredients

- Lemon zest (1 tsp)
- Pistachio (½ cup)
- Almonds (½ cup)
- 1 pinch chili flakes
- Pepper and salt accordingly
- 4 zucchinis, sliced finely
- Cashew nuts (1 cup), soaked overnight
- 4 mint leaves
- Olive oil (2 tbsp)
- Lemon juice (2 tbsp)
- 2 garlic cloves
- ½ shallot

Directions

Take a food processor and process shallot along with garlic, olive oil, mint, lemon zest, lemon juice, pepper and salt.

Combine the above mixture with the zucchinis and place on a serving plate.

Mix almonds and pistachio together in a food processor until ground.

Flavor it with pepper, salt as well as chili flakes.

Splash with pasta and serve.

Slow Cooked Roast Chicken

Ingredients

- Whole chicken (4 pounds)
- 4 carrots, peeled and sliced
- Onion powder (1 tsp)
- 2 celery stalk, diced
- Garlic powder (1 tsp)
- Salt (1 tsp)
- Pepper (1 tsp)
- 1 lemon, halved
- Extra virgin olive oil (1 tsp)

Directions

Coat the slow cooker with olive oil.

Take the whole chicken filled with lemon.

Put in the cooker and cook for about 4 hours on high.

Eat and enjoy.

Kale Orange Chicken

Ingredients

- Chicken breast (1 pound), skinless, boneless and cubed
- Orange juice (½ cup)
- Water (½ cup)
- Coconut aminos (¼ cup)
- Flax seeds (3 tbsp)
- Kale (3 cups), chopped
- Sea salt (1 tsp)
- Cracked black pepper (1 tsp)

Directions

Combine all the ingredients in slow cooker and cook for about 4 hours on high heat or 8 hours on low.

Serve!

Spinach And Green Onion Soup

Ingredients

- Spinach leaves (4 cups)
- 1 garlic clove
- 2 green onions
- 1 pinch nutmeg
- Cashew nuts (1 cup), soaked overnight
- Water (1 cup)
- Lemon juice (2 tbsp)
- Lemon zest (1 tbsp)
- Pepper and salt to taste
- Olive oil (2 tbsp)

Directions

Take the blender and blend all the ingredients until smooth.

Transfer the blended mixture to the serving bowl and serve.

Apricot Walnut Chicken

Ingredients

- Extra virgin olive oil (1 tsp)
- Rosemary (1 tsp)

- Sea salt (1 tsp)
- Walnuts (½ cups), chopped
- 6 apricots
- Chicken broth (2 cups)
- Chicken breast (1 pound), skinless, boneless and cubed

Directions

Boil water in a pot and place apricots in it for about 30 seconds.

Remove, peel and quarter.

Coat the slow cooker with olive oil.

Add chicken along with all the ingredients and cook for about 4 hours on high heat.

Exotic Thai Chicken

Ingredients

- Chicken breast (1 pound), boneless, skinless and cubed
- 1 red bell pepper, seeded and sliced
- Frozen green beans (1 cup)
- Full fat canned coconut milk (1 cup)
- Water (1 cup)
- Lemongrass (1 tbsp)
- Curry powder (1 tsp)
- Sea salt (1 tsp)
- Black pepper (1 tsp)

Directions

Mix salt, curry powder, pepper, lemongrass, water and coconut milk together in a bowl.

Now put the chicken along with the green beans in the slow cooker and pour the above mixture over it.

Cook for about 8 hours on high heat.

Eat and enjoy.

Cashew And Tomato Soup

Ingredients

- 4 ripe tomatoes
- ½ celery stalk
- Cashew nuts (½ cup), soaked overnight
- 1 shallot
- 2 garlic cloves
- Water (1 cup)
- ½ lemon, juiced
- Pepper and salt to taste
- Olive oil (2 tbsp)
- Chopped cilantro (2 tbsp)

Directions

Combine tomato, celery, cashews, water, garlic, lemon juice, pepper and salt together in a food processor and process until smooth until smooth.

Transfer it to the serving bowl splash with cilantro and olive oil while serving.

Pumpkin Carrot Soup

Ingredients

- Pumpkin cubes (2 cups)
- Carrot juice (1 cup)
- Water (1 cup)
- Lemon juice (2 tbsp)
- 1 Garlic clove
- 1 small sweet onion
- Turmeric (½ tsp)
- 1 pinch nutmeg
- Extra virgin olive oil (2 tbsp)
- Sesame oil (½ tsp)
- Pepper and salt to taste
- Pumpkin seeds (4 tbsp)

Directions

Take the food processor and process all the ingredients except pumpkin seeds.

Shift the mixture to the serving bowl, splash with pumpkin seeds and then serve.

Spicy Slow-Cooked Chicken Wings

Ingredients

- Chicken wings (2 pounds)
- Red chili flakes (1 tsp)
- Tomato paste (½ can)
- Water (½ cup)
- Maple syrup (½ cup)

- Garlic powder (1 tbsp)
- Cayenne (1 tsp)
- Oregano (1 tsp)

Directions

Mix oregano, cayenne, garlic powder, maple syrup, water, tomato paste and chili flakes together in bowl.

Add chicken to the above mixture and then shift along with the mixture to the slow cooker for cooking.

Cook for about 4 hours and then enjoy eating it.

Tahini Paste And Avocado Soup

Ingredients

- Spinach leaves (1 cup)
- 2 ripe avocados, peeled
- Tahini paste (4 tbsp)
- 1 cucumber
- Water (1 cup)
- 1 garlic clove
- 1 lemon, juiced
- Pepper and salt to taste

Directions

Combine all the ingredients in a food process and process for about 2-3 minutes until creamy and smooth.

Transfer to the serving bowls and splash with cilantro while serving.

Cilantro And Kale Soup

Ingredients

- 1 bunch cilantro
- 1 ripe avocado, peeled
- 1 cucumber
- 1 green onion, chopped
- 1 garlic clove, chopped
- Water (1 ½ cups)
- 4 kale leaves, shredded
- Olive oil (2 tbsp)
- Grated ginger (2 tsp)
- Pepper and salt to taste

Directions

Combine water, cucumber, green onion, avocado, cilantro and garlic in a food processor and process until smooth.

Transfer the above mixture into the serving bowl and reserve.

Take a separate bowl and combine kale along ginger and olive oil.

Season to taste with pepper and salt.

Place on the top of the soup while serving.

Cucumber And Cashew Soup

Ingredients

- 1 cucumber
- Cashew nuts (1 cup), soaked overnight
- 4 mint leaves

- Water (1 ½ cups)
- Lemon juice (2 tbsp)
- 1 garlic clove
- Pepper and salt to taste

Directions

Blend all the ingredients in a blender until smooth and then serve fresh.

Lime Avocado Soup

Ingredients

- 2 ripe avocados, peeled
- ½ cucumber
- ½ celery stalk
- 1 handful fresh coriander
- Cumin powder (¼ tsp)
- Water (1 cup)
- Coconut milk (1 ½ cups)
- Coconut flesh (¼ cup)
- 2 limes, juiced
- Pepper and salt to taste
- Chopped chives (2 tbsp)

Directions

Combine cucumber along with avocados, celery stalk, coriander, cumin powder, water, coconut milk, coconut flesh and lime juice together in a blender and blend until smooth.

Flavor to taste with pepper and salt.

Pour into the serving bowl and splash with chopped chives before serving.

Broccoli Soup

Ingredients

- Broccoli florets (2 cups)
- ½ avocado
- 1 celery stalk
- 1 garlic clove
- Grated ginger (½ teaspoon)
- Chopped onion (1 tbsp)
- Water (1 cup)
- Almond milk (1 cup)
- 1 ripe tomato, peeled and diced
- Sliced almonds (2 tbsp)
- Pepper and salt to taste

Directions

Combine all the ingredients in a food processor (except tomato and almonds) and process until creamy and smooth.

Pour the mixture to the bowl and splash with sliced almonds and diced tomatoes while serving.

Carrot Ginger Soup

Ingredients

- Fresh carrot juice (1 cup)
- 2 large carrots, sliced
- 1 garlic clove
- Garam masala (1 tsp)
- Grated ginger (1 tsp)
- Tahini paste (1 tbsp)
- 1 small shallot
- Water (2 cups)
- Pepper and salt to taste
- Pumpkin seed oil (2 tbsp)

Directions

Combine shallot, water, tahini paste, ginger, garam masala, carrot juice, garlic and carrot together in a blender and blend for about 2 minutes until smooth.

Flavor it with pepper and salt.

Take serving bowls, shift the above mixture and drizzle with pumpkin seed oil.

Cauliflower And Apple Soup

Ingredients

- 1 head cauliflower
- Chives (1 tbsp)
- 1 small sweet onion
- 1 garlic clove

- Vinegar (1 tsp)
- Raw honey (½ tsp)
- Water (1 cup)
- Olive oil (4 tbsp)
- 2 green apples, peeled and cored
- Pepper and salt according to taste

Directions

Process all the ingredients in a food processor and shift to the serving bowl while serving.

Brussels Sprout Casserole

Ingredients

- Brussels sprouts (2 pounds), quartered
- 2 protobello mushrooms, sliced
- 2 green onions, chopped
- 1 lemon, juiced
- Raw honey (2 tbsp)
- Dried cranberries (½ cup)
- Sliced almonds (1 cup)
- Pepper and salt to taste
- Olive oil (2 tbsp)
- Coconut aminos (2 tbsp)

Directions

Combine all the ingredients together in a serving bowl and stir until coated evenly.

Serve!

Cauliflower With Curry Sauce

Ingredients

- 1 head cauliflower, cut into florets
- 1 young zucchini
- Curry powder (1 tsp)
- Cashews (¼ cup), soaked overnight
- Lemon juice (2 tbsp)
- Turmeric (½ tsp)
- Garlic powder (1 tsp)
- Onion powder (1 tsp)
- Smoked paprika (½ tsp)
- Coconut milk (¼ cup)
- Olive oil (2 tbsp)
- Pepper and salt to taste

Directions

Combine curry powder along with zucchini, lemon juice, cashews, turmeric, onion, powder, garlic powder, coconut milk, paprika, olive oil, salt and pepper in a blender and blend until smooth.

Take the cauliflower florets, pour the above mixture over it and mix gently to coat.

Serve, eat and enjoy.

Paleo Desserts

Strawberry Chocolate Popsicles

Ingredients

- Strawberries (2 cups)
- 2 ripe bananas
- Coconut milk (2 cups)
- Cashew nuts (½ cup), soaked overnight
- Cocoa powder (¼ cup)
- Vanilla extract (1 tsp)
- 1 pinch salt
- Raw honey (¼ cup)

Directions

Take a blender and combine all the ingredients in it.

Blend well and then transfer the mixture into the Popsicle molds.

Chill in the refrigerator for about 2 hours.

Then take out and put into the hot water few minutes while removing the popsicles from their molds.

Serve and enjoy.

Banana Frozen Treats

Ingredients

- 2 large bananas, cut into half
- Dark chocolate (5 ounces)
- Chopped walnuts (½ cup)

Direction

Place skewers in each banana half and chill in the refrigerator for about 2 hours.

Take out and dip in the melted chocolate.

Now roll through walnuts and then serve.

Banana And Coconut Bars

Ingredients

For Crust

- Shredded coconut (½ cup)
- Cashews (1 cup), soaked overnight
- Dates (1 cup), pitted
- Coconut milk (¼ cup)
- 1 pinch nutmeg

For Filling

- 2 ripe bananas
- Almond butter (½ cup)
- Coconut milk (¼ cup)

- Raw honey (4 tbsp)
- Coconut flakes (1 cup)
- Coconut oil (¼ cup)
- Vanilla extract (1 tsp)

Directions

Mix cashews with shredded coconut, dates, coconut milk and nutmeg together in a food processor and process until smooth.

Line the baking pan with plastic wrap and shift the above mixture into it. Set aside.

Mix almond butter, bananas, raw honey, coconut milk, coconut flakes, vanilla extract and coconut oil together in a food processor and process to make filling.

Scatter the mixture over the crust and chill in the refrigerator for about 2 hours.

Then take out, cut into bars and serve.

Cinnamon Fruit Pancakes

Ingredients

- 2 ripe bananas
- Ground flax seeds (2 cups)
- Raw honey (2 tbsp)
- Cinnamon powder (½ tsp)
- Ground ginger (½ tsp)
- 1 pinch of salt
- Fresh strawberries (2 cups)

Directions

Combine raw honey along with bananas, flax seeds, salt, ginger and cinnamon together.

Take a baking sheet and spread the above mixture into small circles on it.

Let it stand for few hours in a warm and dry place and then top with fresh strawberries while serving.

Cashew And Date Pudding

Ingredients

- Dates (1 cup), pitted
- Cashews (1 ½ cups), soaked overnight
- Water (¼ cup)
- Raw honey (¼ cup)
- 1 pinch nutmeg
- Cinnamon powder (½ tsp)
- Raw cocoa powder (2 tbsp)
- 1 pinch of salt

Directions

Combine all the ingredients in a food processor and process until smooth.

Then shift the mixture to the serving bowl and serve.

Chocolate Pecan Pie

Ingredients

For Crust

- Raw almonds (½ cup)
- Pecans (1 cup)
- Dates (1 cup), pitted
- 1 pinch of salt,
- 1 pinch nutmeg
- Vanilla extract (1 tsp)

For Filling

- 2 ripe avocado, peeled
- Lemon juice (2 tbsp)
- Cashews (½ cup), soaked overnight
- Coconut milk (½ cup)
- Dates (½ cup), pitted
- Raw honey (¼ cup)
- Raw cocoa powder (¼ cup)
- 1 pinch salt

Directions

Process all the ingredients in a food processor until ground.

Shift mixture to the pie pan, press it down and reserve.

Mix lemon juice along with avocados, cashews, coconut milk, dates, cocoa powder and raw honey in a food process to make filling.

Then pour into the crust and chill for about 60 minutes before serving.

Strawberry Tart

Ingredients

For Crust

- Almonds (2 cups)
- Cashews (½ cup), soaked overnight
- Raw honey (2 tbsp)
- 1 pinch salt
- Vanilla extract (1 tsp)
- Dates (½ cup), pitted

For Filling

- Fresh strawberries (4 cups), halved

Directions

Mix all the ingredients (except strawberries) together in a food processor and process until smooth.

Shift the mixture to the tart pan and press well.

Top with strawberries and chill for about 60 minutes and then serve.

Avocado Chocolate Mousse

Ingredients

- 2 ripe avocados, peeled
- Raw cocoa powder (¼ cup)
- Coconut cream (1 cup)
- Raw honey (¼ cup)

- 1 pinch of salt
- Vanilla extract (1 tsp)

Directions

Mix all the ingredients in a food processor and process until well mixed.

Shift to the serving bowl and chill for about 2 hours in the refrigerator and then serve.

Chia Raspberry Pudding

Ingredients

- Fresh raspberries (2 cups)
- Raw honey (2 tbsp)
- Chia seeds (¼ cup)
- Lemon juice (1 tsp)

Directions

Mix lemon juice along with raw honey and raspberries in a food processor and process.

Transfer the mixture into a serving bowl and put in chia seeds.

Let it stand for some time to cool and then serve.

Sticky Toffee Pudding Cake

Ingredients

For Cake

- Raw Coconut flour (1 cup)
- Ground flax seeds (½ cup)

- Raw sprouted buckwheat flour (1 cup)
- Cinnamon powder (½ tsp)
- Ground cloves (½ tsp)
- 1 pinch salt
- Agave syrup (¼ cup)
- Vanilla extract (1 tsp)
- Pumpkin puree (1 ½ cups)
- Medjool dates (1 cup), pitted

For Caramel

- Medjool dates (1 cup)
- Coconut butter (1 ¼ cup)
- Raw honey (¼ cup)
- 1 pinch of salt
- Water (2 tbsp)

Directions

First of all to make a cake, combine all the ingredients in a food processor and process until well mixed.

Line round cake pan with plastic wrap and pour the above mixture in it and freeze for about half hour.

Now to make caramel, combine all the ingredients together in a food processor and process until smooth.

Take out the cake from the pan, splash with caramel and serve.

Chocolate Covered Figs

Ingredients

- Dark chocolate chips (1 cup)
- 10 walnuts halves
- 10 figs

Directions

Melt chocolate chips.

Stuff figs with walnuts and then dip in the melted chocolate chips.

Shift the above mixture into the baking sheet and let it cool for about 10 minutes before serving.

Apple Cobbler

Ingredients

For Crust

- Apples (2 pounds), peeled and diced
- 1 lemon, juiced
- Lemon zest (2 tbsp)
- Raw honey (¼ cup)

For Topping

- Almonds (1 cup)
- Walnuts (1 cup)
- Coconut oil (2 tbsp)
- Vanilla extract (2 tbsp)
- Raw honey (2 tbsp)
- 1 pinch salt

Directions

Mix apples, juice, lemon zest and raw honey together in a bowl and marinade for about half hour.

Transfer the above mixture to the deep serving bowl and reserve until the topping are ready.

Now mix almonds, walnuts, coconut oil, vanilla extract, salt and raw honey together in a blender to make topping.

Spread the above mixture over apples and then serve.

Avocado Key Lime Pie

Ingredients

For Crust

- Almonds (1 cup)
- Walnuts (1 cup)
- Dates (1 cup), pitted
- Lemon juice (2 tbsp)
- Raw honey (2 tbsp)
- Coconut oil (2 tbsp)
- 1 pinch of salt

For Filling

- 2 ripe avocados, peeled
- 4 key limes, juiced
- 4 lemon zest
- Cashews nuts (2 cups), soaked overnight
- Raw honey (½ cup)
- 1 pinch salt
- Vanilla extract (1 tsp)

Directions

Mix dates, lemon, walnuts, almonds, lemon juice, raw honey, salt and coconut oil together in a food process and process until smooth.

Shift the above mixture to the pie pan, press well and set aside.

Now combine avocado along with cashews together in a blender and blend until smooth.

Put in raw honey, salt, vanilla, lime juice and zest and then pour into the crust.

Chill for about 60 minutes before serving.

Chocolate Cookie Squares

Ingredients

For Crust

- Almonds (1 cup)
- Cashews (1 cup), soaked overnight
- Agave syrup (2 tbsp)
- Dark chocolate chips (1 cup)

For Topping

- Cocoa powder (½ cup)
- Coconut oil (1 cup)
- Raw honey (¼ cup)
- Coconut cream (¼ cup)
- 1 pinch salt
- Vanilla extract

Directions

Take a small baking pan lined with plastic wrap.

Mix almonds, cashews, agave syrup and chocolate chips together and pour into the baking pan.

Set aside.

Mix coconut oil, raw honey, cocoa powder, vanilla extract, salt and coconut cream together and pour it over crust mixture.

Chill in the refrigerator for about 2 hours and then cut into squares while serving.

Blueberry Mini Pies

Ingredients

For Crust

- Dates (1 cup), pitted
- Shredded coconut (1 ½ cups)
- Almond flour (1 cup)
- Raw honey (2 tbsp)
- 1 pinch salt

For Filling

- Almond butter (½ cup)
- Ground almonds (1 cup)
- Blueberries (3 cups)
- Coconut oil (½ cup)
- 1 pinch salt
- Raw honey (¼ cup)
- Lemon juice (2 tbsp)
- Lemon zest (1 tbsp)

Directions

Mix dates, salt, raw honey, almond flour, and shredded coconut together in a blender and blend until creamy and smooth.

Take about 12 small pie tins, shift the above mixture to these pie tins and set aside.

Take a blender and blend blueberries along with the almond butter, ground almonds, lemon juice, honey, salt, coconut oil and lemon zest together.

Pour the filling over crust and chill for about 60 minutes before serving.

Frozen Cashew And Mango Bites

Ingredients

For Crust

- Dates (1 cup), pitted
- Shredded coconut (1 ½ cups)
- Almond flour (1 cup)
- Raw honey (2 tbsp)
- 1 pinch salt

For Filling

- Almond butter (½ cup)
- Ground almonds (1 cup)
- Blueberries (3 cups)
- Coconut oil (½ cup)
- 1 pinch salt
- Raw honey (¼ cup)
- Lemon juice (2 tbsp)
- Lemon zest (1 tbsp)

Directions

Combine shredded coconut, dates, almond flour, salt and honey in a food processor and process until smooth.

Then shift to the small pie tin, press well and set aside.

Take a blender and put in lemon juice along with lemon zest, honey, salt, coconut oil, ground almonds, butter and blueberries together and blend to make filling.

Then pour this filling into mini pie and chill for about 60 minutes in the refrigerator before serving.

Pumpkin Dark Chocolate Fudge

Ingredients

- Pumpkin puree (1 cup)
- Cashews (1 cup), soaked overnight
- Dates (½ cup)
- 1 pinch of salt
- Raw honey (¼ cup)
- Cinnamon powder (1 tsp)
- Coconut cream (1 tsp)
- Cocoa powder (¼ cup)
- Coconut oil (¼ cup)
- Vanilla extract (1 tsp)

Directions

Put all the ingredients in a food processor and process until creamy and smooth.

Line baking dish with plastic wrap and pour the above mixture in it.

Chill for about 2 hours in the refrigerator.

Then take out, cut into small cubes and serve.

Coconut Goji Berry Truffles

Ingredients

- Coconut butter (½ cup), melted
- Shredded coconut (1 cup)
- Goji berries (¼ cup), chopped
- Raw honey (2 tbsp)
- 1 pinch salt

Directions

Combine honey, salt, berries, shredded coconut and butter together in a food processor and process until well mixed.

Leave the mixture for few minutes to firm slightly and then form small balls of it.

Place the balls on the candy papers and chill in the refrigerator before serving.

Spicy Dark Chocolate Truffles

Ingredients

- Vanilla extract (1 tsp)
- 1 pinch chili flakes
- Coconut cream (½ cup)
- Raw honey (¼ cup)

- Raw cocoa powder (1 cup)
- Coconut oil (1 cup), melted
- Cocoa powder for rolling (¼ cup)

Directions

Blend all the ingredients together and chill for about 20 minutes.

Take out the mixture and form small balls of it.

Roll through powder before serving.

Chocolate Chip Energy Bars

Ingredients

- Ground walnuts (½ cup)
- Vanilla extract (1 tbsp)
- Almond flour (2 cups)
- Dark chocolate chips (1 cup)
- 1 pinch salt
- Coconut oil (¼ cup)
- Raw honey (½ cup)
- Almond butter (½ cup)
- Shredded coconut (1 cup)

Directions

Combine vanilla, raw honey, almond butter and coconut oil in a blender and blend.

Put in salt, shredded coconut, walnuts, chocolate chips and almond butter and shift to baking pan.

Chill for about an hour in the refrigerator and cut into squares before serving.

7-Days Diet Plan For Beginners

Day 1	
Breakfast	Spinach Omelet
Lunch	Chicken Spicy Rice
Salad	Spicy Tuna Salad
Dinner	Brussels Sprout Casserole
Dessert	Strawberry Chocolate Popsicles
Day 2	
Breakfast	Eggplant With Eggs
Lunch	Spinach Tart
Salad	Avocado Tuna Salad
Dinner	Spicy Slow-Cooked Chicken Wings
Dessert	Cashew And Date Pudding

Day 3	
Breakfast	Paleo Breakfast Stir Fry Recipe
Lunch	Meaty Cauliflower Lasagna
Salad	Chicken Taco Salad
Dinner	Tahini Paste And Avocado Soup
Dessert	Chia Raspberry Pudding
Day 4	
Breakfast	Scrambled Eggs With Chili
Lunch	Hawaiian Pineapple Chicken
Salad	Delicious Slaw
Dinner	Pumpkin Carrot Soup
Dessert	Apple Cobbler
Day 5	
Breakfast	Spicy India Omelet
Lunch	Lettuce And Cucumber Soup

Salad	Creamy Carrot Salad
Dinner	Kale Orange Chicken
Dessert	Blueberry Mini Pies

Day 6

Breakfast	Spectacular Spinach Omelet
Lunch	Pomegranate Ginger Chicken
Salad	Asian Aspiration Salad
Dinner	Mint Zucchini Pasta With Pistachio Crumble
Dessert	Spicy Dark Chocolate Truffles

Day 7

Breakfast	Spicy Spinach Bake
Lunch	Vegetarian Curry With Squash
Salad	Sweet Apple Coleslaw
Dinner	Sweet Potato Spiced Soup

Dessert	Strawberry Tart

Conclusion

Despite having such a busy life and living in a such a polluted world, we can still build our own island of healthiness by choosing the best life style for us; a lifestyle that brings with it as many benefits as possible, that provides us with plenty of nutrients, and that is not restrictive at all.

Paleo fits into all of these categories and offers us a solution to become healthy – this doesn't include just us, but our entire family, from grown-ups to kids; we can all benefit from such a nutritious diet.

This book helped you to have a better understanding of the paleo diet. The purpose of this book was to guide paleo beginners and to show them how easy it is to follow paleo lifestyle. There is no specific formula which shows you exactly that when and how much you have to eat. Paleo as a diet and lifestyle choice is all about following your own paleo code, which you will be able to form once you have settled into the diet and feel confident enough to take charge of your paleo journey. But for the beginners I set 1-week diet plan.

If you follow this weekly diet plan and try the recipes I shared with you, I assure you that you will see a better and healthier you in no time.

So take action, put your apron on, head to the kitchen, stay committed, dedicated to your goals and enjoy your new lifestyle with paleo. Good luck!

About The Author

Alisha Abbott is an experienced chef & Author. She is a food columnist and conducted cooking classes.

She like to prepare nutritional meals due to the fact from the beginning she has grow to be a lot more knowledgeable about how the foodstuff we consume has an effect on our health and wellness, therefore she has picked to be effective on personal cooking from the beginning and attempt to put together much healthier and straightforward dishes for her loved ones.

She truly tend not to do other things aside from cooking & exploring brand new, extremely versatile and mouth-watering dishes. She really hope to share her personal wonderfully and balanced mouth-watering food dishes with you as well plus they become the perfect all-time darling dishes.

Printed in Great Britain
by Amazon